bush theatre

The Bush Theatre presents the world premiere of

St Petersburg

by Declan Feenan

6 – 25 October 2008

Cast

The Boy	**Zac Bann-Murray**
	Bradley Ford
John	**Geoffrey Hutchings**
Kate	**Mairead McKinley**
Director	**James Grieve**
Designer	**Lucy Osborne**
Lighting Designer	**Natasha Chivers**
Sound Designer	**Emma Laxton**
Composer	**Arthur Darvill**
Assistant Director	**Hannah Ashwell-Dickinson**
Company Stage Managers	**Rebekah Kirk**
	Angela Riddell
Assistant Stage Manager	**Charlotte Heath**

The Bush Theatre would like to give particular thanks to AKA and to Richard Lee and The Jerwood Space, and would like to thank The Brook Green Hotel, The Defector's Weld, The Stinging Nettle, Zeeta Jacobs at Chicken Shed Theatre Company, and the New London Performing Arts Centre.

JERWOOD **SPACE**   aka

St Petersburg received its world premiere on 6 October 2008.

Zac Bann-Murray The Boy

Zac attends the Barbara Speake Stage School in East Acton, where he has been a student for the past three years.

Theatre includes: the launch of Disney's *High School Musical 2*.

TV includes: *The Bill, Toonattik, The Omid Djalili Show, New Tricks*.

Bradley Ford The Boy

Bradley is currently training at Ravenscourt Theatre School.

Theatre includes: *Billy Elliot* (Victoria Palace); *2000 Feet Away* (The Bush).

Film includes: *V for Vendetta, Rush Hour*.

Geoffrey Hutchings John

Geoffrey trained at RADA and is an Associate Artist of the Royal Shakespeare Company. Work with the Royal Shakespeare Company includes: *Julius Caesar, The Duchess of Malfi, 'Tis Pity She's a Whore, Henry V, All's Well That Ends Well, Twelfth Night, The Winter's Tale, A Midsummer Night's Dream, The Two Gentlemen of Verona*. Work with the National Theatre includes: *Jacobowsky and the Colonel, Three Men and a Horse, The Shaughraun, Mother Courage, Flight, Cleo, Camping, Emmanuelle and Dick, The Riot, Luther*. Other theatre includes: *The Lady from the Sea* (Almeida); *Endgame* (Albery); *The Birthday Party* (Duchess); *Cabaret* (Lyric).

TV includes: *Benidorm, Cor Blimey, The Hogfather, Foyle's War, Kavanagh QC, Goodnight Mister Tom, Henry IV, Our Friends in the North, Maigret, Bye Bye Baby*.

Film includes: *It's All About Love, Mike Bassett – England Manager, Topsy-Turvy, Wish You Were Here, Heart of Darkness, Henry V*.

Mairead McKinley Kate

Mairead trained at RADA, where she won the Pauline Siddle Award. Work with the National Theatre includes: *The Hour We Knew Nothing of Each Other, Translations, Cyrano de Bergerac, Fair Ladies at a Game of Poem*. Work with the Royal Shakespeare Company includes: *Roberto Zucco, Shadows of the Glen, Riders to the Sea, Purgatory*. Other theatre includes: *Ten Rounds, Further than the Furthest Thing* (Tricycle); *Macbeth, Don Juan* (West Yorkshire Playhouse); *The Cherry Orchard* (Oxford Stage Company); *The Decameron* (Gate, London); *The Terrible Voice of Satan* (Royal Court); *The Playboy of the Western World* (Royal Exchange); *The Wind in the Willows, The Servant of Two Masters* (Sheffield Crucible); *The Party's Over* (Theatre Royal Northampton); *Dancing at Lughnasa* (Lyric, Belfast); *The Playboy of the Western World* (Ambassadors, Dublin); *Orestes, The Clearing* (TMA Award, Best Actress in a Supporting Role, Shared Experience).

TV includes: *Doctors, Heartbeat, Casualty, The Amazing Mrs Pritchard, Murder Prevention, Peak Practice, Father Ted, Resort to Murder, Life After Birth*.

Film includes: *Molly's Way* (Four Best Actress Awards at Cinemas Tout Ecran Geneva, Ourense Film Festival Spain, Voldiva International Film Festival Chile and the Bogota Film Festival Colombia), *Sundays, Why Not, Velvet Goldmine*.

Film includes: *The Archers, Japanese Gothic Tales, Feelings Under Siege, Evelina*.

Hannah Ashwell-Dickinson Assistant Director

Hannah is currently studying for an MFA in Theatre Directing at Birkbeck College and is on attachment at The Bush.

Theatre for The Bush includes: *Turf* (directed by Anthea Williams).

Assistant directing work includes: *Vassa, A Servant to Two Masters* (RADA); *Marvellous Animals, Saxophone* (Tristan Bates).

Natasha Chivers Lighting Designer

Theatre for Paines Plough includes: *The Straits, Crazy Gary's Mobile Disco, The Drowned World, Mercury Fur, The Small Things, Pyrenees, If Destroyed True, Tiny Dynamite.* Theatre for Frantic Assembly includes: *Othello, Pool (No Water), Dirty Wonderland* (with Brighton Festival), *Peepshow, Hymns, Sell-Out.*

Other theatre includes: *Sunday in the Park with George* (Olivier Award for Best Lighting Design 2007, Wyndhams); *That Face* (Duke of York's, Royal Court); *Statement of Regret* (National Theatre); *Love* (Vesturport, Lyric Hammersmith); *Beyond Belief* (Arts Council Fellowship Award, Carriageworks, Sydney); *The Wolves in the Walls* (National Theatre of Scotland, Tramway, tour, New York); *Home (Glasgow), Mary Stuart* (National Theatre of Scotland); *Playhouse Creatures, Jerusalem* (West Yorkshire Playhouse); *The Glass Cage, Twelfth Night* (Theatre Royal Northampton).

Lighting for dance includes: *Electric Counterpoint* (Christopher Wheeldon, Royal Opera House); *Encore, Greatest Hits* for the Ballet Boyz (Sadlers Wells, tour), and new pieces by Craig Revel-Horwood, Rafael Bonachela and Will Tuckett for *Ballet for the People* (Royal Festival Hall).

Arthur Darvill Composer

Theatre for The Bush includes: *50 Ways to Leave Your Lover, Sing Project.*

Other music and sound credits for theatre include: *Adult Child Dead Child, Bouncers* (Birmingham Crescent Theatre for Stage 2); *Suddenly Last Summer, Timon of Athens, A Doll's House* (RADA); *Stoopud Fucken Animals* (Traverse); *Present: Tense 6, Artefacts, Public Display of Affection* (nabokov); *Crazy Love* (Paines Plough); *Many Roads to Paradise* (sound design, Finborough); *The Frontline* (Shakespeare's Globe).

Arthur is currently working on a musical version of *Been So Long* with Che Walker for the Young Vic Theatre and is an Artistic Associate of The Bush Theatre.

Declan Feenan Writer

Declan was born in Newry, Co. Down. His plays include: *Limbo* (Sneaky Productions, Belfast 2005, Real Circumstance with York Theatre Royal 2007/8); *Minsk* (Bush Theatre Shorts, Latitude Festival 2007, Mind The Gap NY 2008); and *Lough* (Real Circumstance with York Theatre Royal 2008). He has been on attachment at the National Theatre, London.

James Grieve Director

James is associate director of The Bush and artistic director of nabokov.

Theatre for nabokov includes: *Artefacts* (The Bush, national tour, Off-Broadway), *Kitchen, Bedtime for Bastards, Nikolina, Old Street*.

James trained as assistant and associate director to Josie Rourke, as staff director to Howard Davies on *Philistines* and *Present Laughter* at the National Theatre, and on the National Theatre Studio Directors' Course.

Emma Laxton Sound Designer

Theatre for The Bush includes: *2000 Feet Away, Tinderbox*.

Theatre for the Royal Court includes: *That Face, Gone Too Far!, Catch, Scenes from the Back of Beyond, Woman and Scarecrow, The World's Biggest Diamond, Incomplete and Random Acts of Kindness, My Name Is Rachel Corrie* (also Minetta Lane, New York, Galway Festival, Edinburgh Festival), *Bone, The Weather, Bear Hug, Terrorism, Food Chain*. West End theatre includes: *That Face* (Duke of York's); *My Name Is Rachel Corrie* (Playhouse Theatre).

Other theatre includes: *Pornography* (Traverse, Birmingham Rep); *Welcome to Ramallah* (Ice and Fire); *Shoot/Get Treasure/Repeat* (National Theatre); *Europe* (Dundee Rep, Barbican Pit); *Other Hands* (Soho); *The Unthinkable* (Sheffield Theatres); *My Dad is a Birdman* (Young Vic); *The Gods are Not to Blame* (Arcola); *Late Fragment* (Tristan Bates).

Lucy Osborne Designer

Lucy graduated from the Motley Theatre Design School.

Theatre for The Bush includes: *2000 Feet Away, Tinderbox, Artefacts, tHe dYsFUnCKshOnalZ!*.

Other theatre includes: *Macbeth* (Edinburgh Lyceum, Nottingham Playhouse); *Be My Baby* (New Vic, Stoke); *Some Kind of Bliss* (Trafalgar Studios); *Rope* (Watermill Theatre); *Closer* (Northampton Theatre Royal); *Touch Wood* (Stephen Joseph); *Breaker Morant* (Edinburgh Festival 2007); *Ship of Fools* (set, Theatre503); *The Long and the Short and the Tall* (Sheffield Lyceum, tour); *Dr Faustus* (The Place); *Richard III* (Cambridge Arts Theatre); *The Tempest* (set, Box Clever national tour); *The Prayer Room* (Edinburgh International Festival, Birmingham Rep); *Flight Without End, Othello, Lysistrata* (LAMDA); *Season of Migration to the North* (RSC New Work Festival); *Almost Blue* (Oxford Samuel Beckett Trust Award, Riverside Studios); *The Unthinkable* (Sheffield Crucible Studio); *Generation* (Gate, London).

The Bush Theatre

The Bush Theatre is a world-famous home for new plays and an internationally renowned champion of playwrights. We discover, nurture and produce the best new playwrights from the widest range of backgrounds, and present their work to the highest possible standards. We look for exciting new voices that tell contemporary stories with wit, style and passion and we champion work that is both provocative and entertaining.

The Bush has produced hundreds of groundbreaking premieres since its inception 36 years ago. The theatre produces up to eight productions of new plays a year, many of them Bush commissions, and hosts guest productions by leading companies and artists from all over the world.

The Bush is widely acclaimed as the seedbed for the best new playwrights, many of whom have gone on to become established names in the entertainment industry, including Helen Blakeman, Amelia Bullmore, Richard Cameron, David Eldridge, Kevin Elyot, Jonathon Harvey, Dusty Hughes, Terry Johnson, Charlotte Jones, Dennis Kelly, Doug Lucie, Sharman Macdonald, Conor McPherson, Chloë Moss, Mark O'Rowe, Joe Penhall, Stephen Poliakoff, Philip Ridley, Billy Roche and Snoo Wilson. We also champion the introduction of new talent to the industry, whilst continuing to attract major acting and directing talents, including Frances Barber, Kate Beckinsale, Jim Broadbent, Simon Callow, Brian Cox, Lindsay Duncan, Joseph Fiennes, Mike Figgis, Patricia Hodge, Jane Horrocks, Bob Hoskins, Mike Leigh, Mike Newell, Stephen Rea, Alan Rickman, Tim Roth, Nadim Sawalha, Anthony Sher, John Simm, Alison Steadman, Julie Walters, Richard Wilson and Victoria Wood.

The Bush has won over one hundred awards, and developed an enviable reputation for touring its acclaimed productions nationally and internationally. Recent tours and transfers include the West End production of *Elling* (2007), the West End transfer and national tour of *Whipping It Up* (2007), a national tour of *Mammals* (2006), an international tour of *After the End* (2005-6), *adrenalin... heart* representing the UK in the Tokyo International Arts Festival (2004), the West End transfer (2002) and national tour of *The Glee Club* (2004), a European tour of *Stitching* (2003), and Off-Broadway transfers of *Howie the Rookie* and *Resident Alien*. Film adaptations include *Beautiful Thing* and *Disco Pigs*.

The Bush Theatre provides a free script-reading service, receiving over 1000 scripts through the post every year, and reading and responding to every one. This is one small part of a comprehensive playwrights' development programme which nurtures the relationship between writer and director, as well as playwright residencies and commissions. Everything that we do to develop playwrights focuses them towards a production on our stage or beyond. We have also launched an ambitious new education, training and professional development programme, **bush**futures, providing opportunities for different sectors of the community and professionals to access the expertise of Bush playwrights, directors, designers, technicians and actors, and to play an active role in influencing the future development of the theatre and its programme.

The Bush Theatre is extremely proud of its reputation for artistic excellence, its friendly atmosphere, and its undisputed role as a major force in shaping the future of British theatre.

Josie Rourke
Artistic Director

At The Bush Theatre

Artistic Director	**Josie Rourke**
General Manager	**Angela Bond**
Associate Director bushfutures	**Anthea Williams**
Associate Director	**James Grieve**
Finance Manager	**Viren Thakker**
Marketing Manager	**Alix Hearn**
Production Manager	**Sam Craven-Griffiths**
Assistant Producer	**Caroline Dyott**
Acting Development Manager	**Chantelle Staynings**
Artists' Administrator	**Tara Wilkinson**
Box Office Supervisor	**Clare Moss**
Box Office Assistants	**Natasha Bloor** **Kirsty Cox** **Ava Leman Morgan**
Front of House Duty Managers	**Kellie Batchelor** **Alex Hern** **Ava Leman Morgan** **Glenn Mortimer** **Sam Plumb** **Rose Romain** **Lois Tucker**
Duty Technicians	**Deb Jones** **Sara Macleod** **George Maddocks** **Ben Sherratt** **Clare Spillman** **Shelley Stace** **Matthew Vile**
Associate Artists	**Tanya Burns** **Arthur Darvill** **Chloe Emmerson** **James Farncombe** **Richard Jordan** **Emma Laxton** **Paul Miller** **Lucy Osborne**
Associate Playwright	**Anthony Weigh**
Creative Associates	**Nathan Curry** **Charlotte Gwinner** **Clare Lizzimore** **George Perrin** **Hamish Pirie** **Dawn Walton**
Writer in Residence	**Jack Thorne**
Press Representative	**Ewan Thomson**
Resident Assistant Director	**Hannah Ashwell-Dickinson**
Intern	**Natasha Bloor**

The Bush Theatre
Shepherd's Bush Green
London W12 8QD

Box Office: 020 8743 5050
www.bushtheatre.co.uk

The Alternative Theatre Company Ltd. (The Bush Theatre)
is a Registered Charity number: 270080
Co. registration number 1221968 | VAT no. 228 3168 73

supported by

Be there at the beginning

Our work identifying and nurturing playwrights is only made possible through the generous support of our Patrons and other donors. Thank you to all those who have supported us during the last year.

If you are interested in finding out how to be involved, please visit the 'Support Us' section of www.bushtheatre.co.uk, or call 020 8743 3584.

Lone Star
Gianni Alen-Buckley
Princess of Darkness
Catherine & Pierre Lagrange

Handful of Stars
Joe Hemani
Sarah Phelps

Glee Club
Anonymous
Judith Bollinger
Jim Broadbent
Clyde Cooper
David & Alexandra Emmerson
Sophie Fauchier
Albert & Lyn Fuss
Piers & Melanie Gibson
Tanny Gordon
Jacky Lambert
Richard & Elizabeth Philipps
Paul & Jill Ruddock
John & Tita Shakeshaft
June Summerill
Charles Wansbrough

Beautiful Thing
Anonymous
Mrs Oonagh Berry
John Bottrill
Seana Brennan
Alan Brodie
Kate Brooke
David Brooks
Maggie Burrows
Clive Butler
Justin Coldwell
Alex Gammie
Vivien Goodwin
Sheila Hancock
Lucy Heller
Francis & Mary-Lou Hussey
Virginia Ironside
The Violet Crème
Adam Kenwright
Kim Lavery
Antonia Lloyd
Ligeia Marsh
Kirsty Mclaren
Michael McCoy

Tim McInnerny & Annie Gosney
Judith Mellor
David & Anita Miles
Mr & Mrs Philip Mould
John & Jacqui Pearson
Mr & Mrs A Radcliffe
Wendy Rawson
John Reynolds
Caroline Robinson
Nadim Sawalha
Barry Serjent
Brian D Smith
Mrs Peter Templeton
Abigail Uden

Rookies
Anonymous
Tony Allday
Pauline Asper Management
Mr and Mrs Badrichani
Veronica Baxter
Tanya Burns & Sally Crabb
Geraldine Caulfield
Sarah Crowley
Alan Davidson
Joy Dean
Camilla Emson
Karen Germain
Carol Ann Gill
Sally Godley
Miranda Greig
Peter Grundy
Jenny Hall
Sian Hansen
Andy Herrity
Mr G Hopkinson
Rebecca Hornby
Joyce Hytner, ACT IV
Hardeep Kalsi
Robin Kermode
Vincent Luck
Ray Miles
Toby Moorcroft – Sayle Screen
Georgia Oetker
Mr & Mrs Malcolm Ogden
Andrew Peck
Julian & Amanda Platt
Radfin Courier Service
Radfin Antiques
Volinka Reina
Clare Rich

Mark Roberts
Martin Shenfield
Johanna Schmitz
John Trotter
Francis Von Hurter
Geoffrey Whight
Alison Winter

Platinum Corporate Members
Anonymous

Silver Corporate Members
The Agency (London) Ltd
Harbottle & Lewis LLP
United Agents

Bronze Corporate Members
Act Productions Ltd
Artists Rights Group
Hat Trick Productions
Orion Management

Trust and foundation supporters
The John S Cohen Foundation
The Earls Court and Olympia Charitable Trust
The Ernest Cook Trust
Garfield Weston Foundation
The Girdlers' Company Charitable Trust
Haberdashers' Benevolent Foundation
Jerwood Charitable Foundation
The John Thaw Foundation
The Kobler Trust
The Laurie & Gillian Marsh Charitable Trust
The Martin Bowley Charitable Trust
The Mercers' Company
The Thistle Trust
The Vandervell Foundation
The Harold Hyam Wingate Foundation
The Peter Wolff Theatre Trust

bushfutures

bushfutures is a groundbreaking programme that allows our community and emerging practitioners and playwrights to access the expertise of Bush writers, directors, designers, technicians and actors.

We are devoted to finding and supporting The Bush artists of tomorrow.

bushfutures **Projects**

bushfutures creates exciting and innovative projects to engage emerging playwrights and produce their plays on The Bush stage. So far in 2008 projects have included **50 Ways to Leave Your Lover** and **The Halo Project**. **50 Ways to Leave Your Lover** was written by five remarkable emerging playwrights and toured to Oxford, Norwich and the Latitude Festival before performing at The Bush Theatre. **The Halo Project** allowed Simon Vinnicombe to work with a large group of young people from Hammersmith and Fulham to develop a new play, **Turf**, which was performed by and for young people in our theatre.

bushfutures **in Schools**

bushfutures develops projects with schools, colleges and tertiary institutions. The Bush is one of Britain's leading New Writing companies. We share our talent and expertise with young people through tailor-made workshops which focus on playwriting, performance and the development of new work.

bushfutures **Associates**

Emerging practitioners make up a group of associates who are an integral part of The Bush community. They are invited to talks and workshops by leading theatre practitioners and involved in development events.

bushtalk

Throughout the year The Bush hosts discussions for the public between leading playwrights and theatre practitioners.

For more information contact **bushfutures@bushtheatre.co.uk**

Declan Feenan

ST PETERSBURG
and other plays

St Petersburg
Limbo
Catherine Medbh

NICK HERN BOOKS
London
www.nickhernbooks.co.uk

For my mother and father

ST PETERSBURG

Characters

JOHN, *elderly*
THE BOY, *around ten*
KATE, *middle-aged*

Setting

A living room in a ground-floor flat.
In the corner there is a bed and on the opposite wall a window.
There is a sideboard. There is a kitchen area.
A door leads off into a bathroom.
A door leads off into the dark hallway – this is always open.

This text went to press before the end of rehearsals and so may differ slightly from the play as performed.

Scene One

Morning.

THE BOY *stands at the window, looking out.*

An ornamental figurine lies smashed on the table.

JOHN *stands over the TV.*

JOHN. Will I see what else is on, will I?

He flicks around the TV.

Do you watch this?
It's a programme that's on.
You see him there – he's a surgeon.
He's performed an operation on that woman's brain.
He was drunk when he did it so the operation all went wrong
– she lost some of her brain.
She isn't dead yet, but she's in a bad state.
And you see her – the one in the red?
That's the surgeon's wife.
She's having an affair with him there.
No not him.
Him.
I only watch it when there's nothing on.
Keeps me occupied.
The stories are ridiculous.
In one episode a plane crashed into the hospital.
How's that for luck?
Some of the acting in it is really bad as well.

JOHN *switches off the TV.*

I'll turn it off.
They'll repeat it on Sunday.

JOHN *begins rummaging in the sideboard.*

I was watching the news last week.

There was a piece on about a dog who could count.

No joke.

They showed him a number on a piece of paper and he'd bark whatever number it was.

Like, he'd bark five times for the number five and seven for seven.

All that kinda nonsense.

A counting dog – on the news.

What's that about?

Nice dog but, y'know, it shouldn't be on the television.

It shouldn't be on the news – should it?

Springer spaniel.

Though he could add and subtract as well, which was impressive.

But you know what I mean – it's not news.

I read a book once – are you listening?

I read a book once.

Not the whole book.

Actually it was more a magazine than a book.

There was a bit about dogs.

Not counting dogs now, just normal dogs.

Dogs in general.

And they know this – I don't know how they know.

They've done research or something – somehow they know.

Dogs are seventy-four times more sensitive to emotions than humans.

Emotional vibrations – you know?

As in when you're sad, when you're happy, whatever.

Dogs can walk into an empty room and tell when someone has been laughing or when someone has been crying.

Like, you know the way you walk into a room and you know there's been a row?

You know there's been an argument?

You sense it, don't you?

It's like that – except dogs are a hundred times better than us.

It's an animal thing.

Intuition.

And cats can hear colour.
No joke – they can tell the difference between red and blue
just by listening to it.
How's that for a trick?

He finds a spatula/fish slice. He throws it into the sink.

He continues searching.

(*Re: smashed ornament*.) Technically this is your fault.
I should blame this on you and get myself off the hook.
But if she notices the crack I'll take the blame.
Hopefully it won't come to that.
She'll be none the wiser.
It'll be our secret.

He finds a roll of Sellotape. He thinks about it.

He drops the Sellotape back in the drawer and closes it.

He opens a cupboard on the sideboard, searches.

So how's school?
You learning anything?
Tell me something they've taught you.
Tell me something I don't know.
There are three golf balls on the moon.
Did you know that?
You walk into school tomorrow and tell them there are three
golf balls on the moon.
They'll put you to the top of the class.

He searches deeper.

And what about the girls?
Any girls on the scene?
Any wee kisses after school?
Up at the football field behind the dugouts?
Are you getting any of that?
Ah! – good man.
What's her name?
Does she have a name?

JOHN *finds the glue*.

Here we go.
I'll have this fixed in no time.
She'll never know.

He sits at the table and sets about mending the ornament.

What do you think?
Would you like to live in a place like this?
Do you think you could go for a place like this?
It's not too bad once you get used to it.
There's fellas living in cardboard boxes – sleeping on park benches and that.
And here's me in the warm and dry.
I should count myself lucky, shouldn't I?
You've got to be careful with this stuff. (*Re: glue*.)
It burns you and takes your skin off.
How's that?
You wouldn't know, would you?

JOHN *places the figurine on the sideboard*.

He sets about tidying up the mess.

(*Suddenly*.) And if anyone hits you first, make sure you hit them back!
At least once.
I know that sounds obvious but it's worth saying.
Even if they're bigger than you – even if he's built like a tank.
If he hits you – you hit him back.
Even if he beats you into a pulp.
Because there's a rule.
If you get one swing at him and it connects – you haven't lost.
That's official.
That's a rule.
You haven't won but you haven't lost.
It doesn't matter what it's about.
It doesn't matter who's watching you.
So if he hits you first, give it to him.
Promise me you'll do that.
Good man.

He comes across a small tin box.

I don't believe it.
I don't believe it.

He opens the box. Pause. From the box he takes out an old copybook. He smiles. He begins reading. After a while:

Look at this.
'X plus Y to the power of 3.'
How did I ever get that right?
Look at all that working out there.
How did I ever get that right?
This is what I'm saying to you.
It's all about the smarts.

From the box he takes out a prayer book, a toy car and a fishing reel.

Pause. He tidies everything away back into the sideboard except for the box and its contents.

Why did I keep this, do you think?
What did I think I was going to do with it?
No medals though, huh?
Men my age should have a medal or two.
Or a trophy.
Or something.

He puts the box under the pillow.

Over the following he takes the picture of the lighthouse and the mirror from the wall, one at a time, and shoves them down the back of the sideboard.

It's getting dark in the afternoons now – have you noticed that?
It won't be long until Christmas now.
That town'll be jammed – the big rush.
They go mad, don't they.
Buying whatever it is they buy.

Pause.

So do you like the snow, young fella?

Plenty of playing done in the snow – snowball fights and all that.

Talking as the master of snowball fighters.

Y'see this arm here?

I could throw a snowball the length of a football field.

No joke.

When I was your age we used to always have a bit of a snowball fight with the fellas up the road.

Making murder – it was great fun.

Once we were at the top of the street waiting to catch the bigger fellas coming around the corner.

We waited and waited but they never came – they were all up in the park making snowmen or something.

We'd a stash of snowballs already made up, ready for throwing but no one to throw them at.

And Mickey only lived across the road from where we were.

And we saw his Da come out of the house.

He was always up for a laugh, you know? – always good for a bit of sport with us.

Mickey gives me the cutest snowball he could find.

He even shines it up nice to make it go faster.

And he gives it to me and I fire it.

We watch it gunning through the air.

But at the same time isn't Mickey's granny coming out of the house?

And she's standing there on the front step carrying a Christmas pudding.

It sounded like somebody punched her in the face.

Pause.

Remember the homeless fella standing outside the cathedral?

He was collecting cardboard and I gave him my cigarette packet?

Where was that?

Pause.

You know what I'm thinking?

Just listen first then tell me if you think it's a good idea.

If you were given a choice to know something or not know
something, you'd want to know, wouldn't you?
If it was about yourself.
If it was about you.
Self-knowledge and all that.
I'm thinking about her mother.
God knows what her mother told her about me.
She'd all that time to fill her head full of rubbish about me.
She's probably told her something about me that she made up.
Out of spite.
Something ridiculous – something mad.
Lies.
Y'know?
I was thinking about telling her something useful.
Something that she'd be able to know herself by.
What do you think?
Do you think that's a good idea?
Me and her mother never planned her.
She came out of the blue.
I was thinking about telling her.
Now I know that might sound a bit cruel – like I'm
punishing her or something.
But I think it would be good for her – to know that.
I do.
It wouldn't change anything.
I was still there at her birth.
That's fact.
Nothing changes that.
And I know it's all in how I say it.
I could just slip it into conversation maybe.
Would that work?
Between talking about… the weather and… hairdressers…
or something.
It's better to know these things.
Best to go through life in the knowledge.
And in the knowledge of how you came into the world in the
first place is a good place to start.
And there wouldn't be anything for her to be disappointed
about.

It could have happened to me for all I know.
But I don't know – and that's what I'm saying.
I would want to know.
If my old fella was here now and he told me that I was an accident, you know what I'd do?
I'd thank him.
I would.
At least you know you were conceived in the heat.
Two people who can't take their hands off each other get carried away in the moment.
That's the way to look at it, isn't it?
Hot and steamy – not planned and tired.

He watches THE BOY.

No one listens to me.
No one gives a shit about what I have to say.
Maybe it's because I'm an old bastard.
Is it that, do you think?
Still, old bastards need to be heard.
There should be a forum for boys like us.
No point in making mistakes twice.
Not if you can help it.
If we didn't learn from other people's mistakes we'd still be living in holes in the ground.
Advancement – that's what it's about.
Passing on the torch, helping people, all of that.

Pause.

Maybe I spent too many days driving in the cold.
In the middle of nowhere.
Maybe that's my problem.

Pause.

What's it like out there?
Let me guess – quiet?
That road used to be humming with cars.
There's hardly any now – the odd one or two maybe.

JOHN *gets up and makes his way over to* THE BOY.

JOHN *reaches to touch* THE BOY'*s head, but doesn't.*

He stares out the window.

Are you still at the fishing?
How's that going?
Catch much?
There's plenty of fish down in the canal there.
It's brimming with roach this time of year.
Do you want to know the secret for catching roach?
Do you want to know the secret for catching roach?
Sweetcorn.
High up on the hook, so it doesn't fall off.
You try that next time and I'll bet you'll net one.
Rutilus rutilus – isn't that it?
It is.
Roach – *rutilus rutilus*.

Scene Two

Early afternoon.

JOHN *is at the window looking out.*

KATE *enters from the hall carrying bags of shopping.*

She dumps everything on the table and settles in – taking off her coat, etc.

JOHN. You get caught in that snow?

KATE. It's gone down my back.

JOHN. It's going to be like that for the rest of the day, they said.

KATE. Did they, yeah?

JOHN. Yeah.

KATE. Doesn't surprise me. It's that type of weather.

JOHN. You didn't get any Wagon Wheels, did you?

KATE. There's an accident at the bottom of the hill there.

JOHN. Is there?

KATE. A gritter crashed into a lamp-post at the bottom of the hill.

JOHN. Crashed?

KATE. Just at the bottom of the hill there. It must have been coming down the hill and hit some ice or something.

JOHN. When was this?

KATE. Just there now. A few minutes ago.

It's hit a lamp-post.

JOHN. That's very dangerous.

KATE. What?

JOHN. Those things are dangerous. They can tip over easily enough.

KATE. Well, no one seems to be hurt. I was going to ask the driver if he was alright but he was on his mobile.

JOHN. Those things can tip over easily enough.

KATE. But you should see the lamp-post, it's all bent over. There's not a scratch on the grit lorry.

JOHN. They weigh about thirteen tonnes when they're full with salt. Fifteen maybe.

KATE. Why don't they put the spreader on the front of those lorries?

JOHN. What do you mean?

KATE. Well, they drive the roads spraying salt out the back of them. Right? But that means the lorry itself is driving on ice, doesn't it? But if they had the spreader at the front, it would mean the lorry is never driving on ice. Do you know what I mean?

JOHN. They're only allowed to drive thirty-seven-and-a-half miles an hour, you know.

KATE. What are?

JOHN. Grit lorries.

KATE. …

JOHN. Thirty-seven-and-a-half miles per hour. Any faster and they're breaking the law.

KATE. …

JOHN. What?

KATE. …

JOHN. You not find that interesting, no?

KATE. Why do I need to know that?

JOHN. I was only saying.

KATE. What do I need to know that for?

JOHN. You don't need to know it.

KATE. …

JOHN. I don't need to know it. No one needs to know it. Weren't we talking? I just thought you'd want to know.

Pause.

Did you get any Wagon Wheels?

KATE. I didn't know you wanted some.

JOHN. I said to you yesterday.

KATE. Did you?

JOHN. Yeah.

KATE. When?

JOHN. I dunno. But I remember saying to you.

KATE. There's ginger nuts there.

JOHN. They've gone soft.

KATE. The ones at the top are soft but the ones underneath will be alright.

KATE takes the ginger nuts, takes one from the middle of the pack and eats it. She suddenly notices.

Where's the picture?

JOHN. I took it down –

KATE. And the mirror?

JOHN. I took it down.

KATE. What for?

JOHN. Just.

KATE. Where did you put it?

JOHN. Behind the sideboard there.

KATE. Did you break it or anything?

JOHN. Do you want it? Take it back if you want.

KATE. No. You might want to put it back up again.

JOHN. …

KATE. Was it because of the cat in it?

JOHN. Cat?

KATE. You know the way you hate cats?

JOHN. …

KATE. So you're just going to leave it like that? Just the bare wall?

JOHN. I like it like that.

Pause.

KATE finishes the biscuit she has, takes another and eats.

KATE. Those weren't too bad.

JOHN. I don't like them when they're soft.

KATE. Don't you soften them in your tea anyway?

JOHN. It's not the same.

KATE takes the pictures from behind the sideboard and places them on the wall.

What are you doing? I don't want them up.

KATE. You can't have the wall bare like that. It makes the place look cold. Now is that straight? I think it is, is it?

Pause.

I can't stay for long today. Thomas has a parent-teacher meeting tonight.

JOHN. Right.

KATE. It starts at half seven but I want to get home and get the dinner on early.

JOHN. Right.

KATE. So I won't be staying long if that's alright? To be honest I'm not looking forward to it. I hate these things.

JOHN. Is he not getting his head down?

KATE. I thought he was. God knows what they're going to say about him. Like he's smart. He's smart and can do anything when he puts his mind to it. But when it comes to school – it's just not his thing, y'know?

JOHN. I thought you said he's good at sums.

KATE. No, that's Mark.

JOHN. Oh right –

KATE. It's Mark you're thinking of.

KATE takes a jumper out of a bag.

What do you think of this?

JOHN. It's nice.

KATE. Here, try it on.

JOHN. It's for me?

KATE. Feel how soft that is. It's real wool too. There's a new shop on Hill Street that's just opened. You know the Reilly's?

JOHN. Who?

KATE. The three Reilly sisters – triplets?

JOHN. No.

KATE. Live out at Damolly?

JOHN. …

KATE. You do. The father's got one hand. A mechanic.

JOHN. No – why?

KATE. They work in it. All three of them.

Pause.

It's real wool. It's nice, isn't it?

JOHN. …

KATE. Take that cardigan off and try it on – see how it looks on you.

JOHN *takes off his cardigan.*

Now put this on you.

JOHN *has trouble with the jumper.* KATE *goes to help him.*

Here, put your arm. Put your arm out. Put your arm. Where's your arm? Put your arm through the sleeve. Put your arm through the sleeve. Now where's your head? Where's your head? Where's your head?

JOHN. My head's where it always is.

KATE. Put your head through – now. There we go. Let's have a look at you.

JOHN. …

KATE. You look smart.

JOHN. …

KATE. Walk up there so I can see it on you.

> JOHN *walks a few paces*.

> Stop scratching at it.

JOHN. It's itchy.

KATE. It's only because it's new. There's a kink at the back. Come here.

> KATE *fixes the jumper on him*.

> Walk up there again.

> JOHN *walks back up the room*.

> Do you like it?

JOHN. It's a bit itchy.

KATE. Apart from that?

JOHN. …

KATE. They've some nice coats in there as well. You'll need a coat if it stays like this.

JOHN. I have a coat already –

KATE. You need a new coat –

JOHN. That's a good warm coat I have –

KATE. We can get you a new one – they weren't that expensive and they had some lovely ones. You can come down with me and pick it out if you want.

JOHN. …

KATE. Stop scratching at it, you'll ruin it! Do you like it?

JOHN. Thanks.

KATE *begins tidying the flat.*

KATE. We had a bit of an incident last night. Turley's horse broke through the fence and wandered into the garden.

JOHN. Your garden?

KATE. Yeah.

JOHN. Yeah?

KATE. Thomas and his friend were out playing on the swing and Thomas lets out a squeal. So I ran out to see what the matter was. And there was Turley's horse standing on the top bank. It had broke through the fence between us and the field.

JOHN *heaves once to clear his chest. He heaves again. Then swallows.*

And anyway it just stood there –

JOHN. Did he run for them?

KATE. Who?

JOHN. The horse.

KATE. Well, that was my first thought. That the horse might rear up or something. But it didn't. It just stood there. It's an old horse, he's had it for years. Still, old or not I had to chase it back –

JOHN *coughs again.*

Are you alright?

JOHN. Hmm.

KATE. I had to chase it back up into the field. I couldn't find the brush so I had to use one of the children's tennis rackets. I must've looked the part, running up the garden in my slippers, chasing a horse with a tennis racket.

JOHN. Sounds like it's all happening in your house!

KATE. That happened before, you know.

JOHN. What?

KATE. A cow broke in – he keeps his cows up in that field as well. Or he hires it out to someone else for their cows – dunno. But the same thing happened with a cow a few years ago.

JOHN. A cow?

KATE. Yeah.

JOHN. I don't trust cows.

KATE. Anyway, when Sean came home from work he had to fix the fence. He wasn't happy. Standing in the dark. Freezing. In the snow. Hammering the post back into the ground.

JOHN. You should say something to him.

KATE. I know.

JOHN. You should say something to him. You've four children running about the house. You can't have cows or horses coming into your garden.

KATE. Imagine if it had stirred up –

JOHN. Well, he's got a responsibilty to keep that fence in good order.

Pause.

KATE. But imagine a black horse standing there in the snow at the top of our garden. It scared the daylights out of me.

Pause.

Sorry I'm a bit late by the way. I was doing a bit of window shopping. I'm looking for one of those standing lamps for the corner of the living room. You know the way we have the sofa out from the wall?

JOHN. Do you?

KATE. Yeah.

JOHN. Right.

KATE. Well, there's that corner of the good room behind the sofa with nothing in it. I thought about getting a plant for there, just to have a bit of green, you know? But it's a bit dark in that corner. So I thought I'll get one of those standing lamps instead. It'll brighten up that side of the room. It'd be nice.

Pause.

Anyway, how are you? You alright?

JOHN. I'm alright, yeah.

KATE. How did you sleep last night?

JOHN. Alright, yeah.

KATE. What do you mean, 'alright'?

JOHN. I woke up a couple of times during the night.

KATE. Did you?

JOHN. Yeah.

KATE. Why, what happened?

JOHN. I don't know. I just woke up.

KATE. …?

JOHN. Just a bit of a sore head.

KATE. Whereabouts?

JOHN. Just at the front there. Just a wee headache.

KATE. Did you take anything for it?

JOHN. I took some paracetamol.

KATE. How many?

JOHN. Two. No, three.

KATE. Three?

JOHN. No, two. Two –

KATE. Because you shouldn't take more than two at a time.

JOHN. I took two then I went back to bed.

KATE. And did you get to sleep after that?

JOHN. Once they kicked in, yeah.

KATE. And what time did you get up?

JOHN. This morning?

KATE. This morning.

JOHN. About half six.

KATE. And did you have breakfast?

JOHN. Aye.

KATE. What did you have?

JOHN. I had some toast with chocolate spread.

KATE. Right –

JOHN. And a cup of tea and a banana.

KATE. And are you feeling alright now?

JOHN. Yeah.

KATE. You sure?

JOHN. Aye. Why?

KATE. You look a bit pale on it.

JOHN. Do I?

KATE. You're a bit dark around the eyes as well.

JOHN. …

KATE. Have you a sore head now?

JOHN. Not really no.

KATE. What do you mean, 'not really'? You either do or you don't.

JOHN. No.

KATE. Maybe it's a head chill or something? And what about your chest?

JOHN. It's alright.

KATE. That's good. Breathing okay then?

JOHN. Yeah.

KATE. And have you finished those tablets yet?

JOHN. I've another two days left.

KATE. Right – well, tell me when they're done, won't you?

KATE *notices a stain on the carpet.*

Did you spill something here?

JOHN. No.

KATE. There's a stain here, look? Maybe it was me – was it?

Pause.

Is it coffee or something? Black coffee?

JOHN. I don't drink coffee.

KATE. Or oil or something?

Pause.

JOHN. How's Sean?

KATE. Alright I think. I haven't seen him in a few days.

JOHN. No?

KATE. He's doing runs to the airport now. He's up at six and he finishes at eight.

JOHN. Is that good?

KATE. It's better paid but it means he finishes late. And he works the weekends as well – Friday night, Saturday day, Saturday night and Sunday night.

JOHN. Right.

KATE. That's what I'm saying to you, I have to go up to this school meeting on my own.

JOHN. But he enjoys the taxiing, though, doesn't he?

KATE. The children miss him.

Silence.

KATE *takes out a handheld vacuum cleaner from her bag.*

(*Re: the vacuum cleaner.*) I brought this.

JOHN. What is it?

KATE. Have you never seen one of these before, no?

JOHN. I have on –

She switches it on and sucks up the pile of dirt. She switches it off.

KATE. It runs on batteries.

JOHN. It's handy, isn't it?

KATE. Have you never seen one before?

JOHN. I have on TV but not in real life.

KATE. Well, this is for you to keep. I have a new one at home.

JOHN. Do you not need it?

KATE. I just bought a new one last week.

KATE *gives it to* JOHN.

You push that switch there and it starts.

JOHN. Ah right.

KATE. Now, what time is it? Do you fancy something to eat – ?

JOHN *switches on the vacuum. He is fascinated. He tests the suction with the palm of his hand.*

It's good, isn't it?

JOHN *turns it off.*

It's good, isn't it?

JOHN. It is good.

KATE. You can keep that. Put it away there where you can find it.

JOHN *puts the vacuum in the sideboard.*

Right. Are you ready for something to eat? There's corned beef there. Or some fish fingers. Or some bacon. Or some soup.

JOHN. What kind of soup is it?

KATE. Farmhouse vegetable. Do you fancy a bowl of farm-house vegetable with a round of bread? Or there's some fish fingers there. Or some bacon.

JOHN. Bacon.

KATE. Will you take a wee bit of bacon, will you?

JOHN. I will.

KATE. A bacon sandwich with a glass of milk?

JOHN. Aye.

KATE. Here, do you want the TV on?

JOHN. No, I'm alright.

KATE. You not want to watch your programmes?

JOHN. No.

KATE. No? Maybe there's some snooker on maybe.

JOHN *goes to the window to look out.*

KATE *sets about frying bacon.*

How's it now? Still coming down?

JOHN. Aye.

KATE. I'd rather walk in fresh snow than old snow. It turns to ice when it's been lying for a while.

Pause.

You spend a lot of time looking out that window. You must miss the outdoors, do you?

JOHN. I like the view.

KATE. What view?

JOHN. The road. And the sky.

KATE. And the roundabout. And the bins.

Pause.

JOHN. I saw the Northern Lights.

KATE. The Northern Lights?

JOHN. Yeah.

KATE. I didn't know you could see them from here.

JOHN. They actually flicker, you know.

KATE. What do you mean?

JOHN. They flicker like a candle. People think they move slowly but they don't. They flicker. The whole way across the sky. Like a film. The whole way across.

KATE. How long ago was this?

JOHN. Yesterday.

KATE. Yesterday?

JOHN. Aye.

KATE. Last night, you mean?

JOHN. No, yesterday afternoon. After you left.

KATE. Are you sure? I thought you could only see them at night.

JOHN. I saw them in the afternoon.

Silence.

KATE. Do those cars out there not annoy you? When they drive past – with their headlights?

JOHN. I don't notice it.

KATE. I suppose you can't hear them either with that double glazing.

Pause.

We did well to get that double glazing – didn't we? It goes to show – if you don't ask, you don't get.

Pause.

JOHN. So you haven't seen much of Sean then?

KATE. No.

JOHN. I like Sean. He's a good fella.

KATE. …

JOHN. Tell him I was asking for him.

KATE. I will if I see him.

Pause.

I met Gerry down the street. He was asking for you. He said he'd take a run up next week to see you.

JOHN. Right.

KATE. He's a grandfather again – did you know that?

JOHN. No.

KATE. Last month. Aisling had another wee girl. That's twenty-three grandchildren he has now.

Pause.

I didn't know Gerry was only in his sixties.

JOHN. Aye.

KATE. I didn't know that.

JOHN. Aye.

KATE. Because I always thought he looked really well, but I thought he was in his eighties. He's not too healthy-looking if he's only, what, sixty-seven, sixty-eight?

JOHN. Something like that.

Pause.

KATE. And what's wrong with his nose?

JOHN. Boxing.

Pause.

KATE. Daddy?

JOHN. Kate?

KATE. I was going through Mum's old stuff last night and I came across a photo.

JOHN. …

KATE. I was going through Mum's old stuff last night and I came across a photo.

JOHN. …

KATE. It was a holiday snap. You, me and Mum. I have it in my bag there if you want to see it?

JOHN. …

KATE. Just for interest. It's a bit ragged but you can make most of it out. I think I must have been about three. I have it in my bag if you want to see it.

Pause.

This bacon smells lovely, doesn't it? It reminds me of a house I used to go to for piano lessons.

JOHN. You?

KATE. Yeah, when I was younger.

JOHN. I didn't know you took piano lessons.

KATE. I haven't played in ages.

JOHN. I didn't know that.

KATE. I did a few exams in it.

JOHN. Were you any good?

KATE. I was alright. I can't play now. If you were to put a piano in front of me now I wouldn't know what to do. I've forgotten it all now.

Pause.

Right. Sit up there – this is ready. Do you want a glass of milk?

JOHN. Yeah.

JOHN *sits at the table.*

KATE. Do you want any sauce?

JOHN. No.

KATE *brings everything to the table.*

KATE. Will I put the radio on?

JOHN. If you want.

They start eating.

KATE. I hope it doesn't snow any more tonight, with me going up to the school.

JOHN. Is the wee fella going with you?

KATE. No. Just me on my own.

JOHN. Are you walking?

KATE. I was thinking about it. But I might have to get a taxi now.

JOHN. You'll be fine.

KATE. Will I?

JOHN. It's only a wee bit of snow.

KATE. You haven't been out walking in it. It's the ice as well more than the snow.

JOHN. When I was growing up, the snow used to be measured in feet, not inches. You hear them saying now about two inches falling and suddenly all the buses stop running and all the trains are cancelled. It's only a couple of inches of snow.

KATE. You wouldn't say that if you were out walking in it. You'd be falling all over the place.

JOHN. I'd be alright.

KATE. Would you, yeah?

JOHN. I've been in colder places than this.

Pause.

KATE. You need your hair cut – it's getting thick. You want me to have a go at it at the weekend?

JOHN. Maybe, aye.

Pause.

KATE. Did you ever drive a grit lorry?

JOHN. Me?

KATE. Yeah.

JOHN. No.

Pause.

KATE. How many miles do you think you've driven?

JOHN. How many?

KATE. Yeah. In your life.

JOHN. It'd be hard to say. I drove to Russia once.

KATE. Did you?

JOHN. Yeah.

KATE. You must have a few stories on you? All that travelling. All those places you've been.

JOHN. ...

KATE. Tell me something then.

JOHN. About what?

KATE. Tell me a story.

JOHN. No.

KATE. Why not?

JOHN. I'm no good at stories.

KATE. I don't believe that –

JOHN. I'm not – I'm no good.

KATE. You used to tell me stories before I went to bed.

JOHN. Aye, but you were a child. I could have told you anything and you would have thought I was the bee's knees.

KATE. Go on, tell me a yarn –

JOHN. I'm no good at stories. I'm telling you.

Pause.

KATE. Did you do your exercises this morning?

JOHN. …

KATE. Did you do your exercises this morning?

JOHN. I did.

KATE. You sure? You want to do them again just so I can see
you?

JOHN. Done them already, I said.

Pause.

KATE. Daddy.

JOHN. …

KATE. Do you want to see it?

*KATE goes to her bag and takes out the photo and puts it in
front of JOHN.*

I still have a few ornaments and a pile of papers as well.
There's no date on it, but I only look about three there,

don't I? I can't be more than three. I think I can remember
that dress I'm wearing. You don't know where it was taken,
do you?

JOHN. ...

KATE. Maybe we were all on holiday or something. It looks
like we're on holiday or something. Doesn't it?

JOHN. ...

KATE. It's my only copy so if you want a copy I can get one
made up –

JOHN. I knew this fella once – are you listening?

KATE. ...

JOHN. Are you listening? A friend of mine was doing a run to
Fermanagh. He was taking a load of brick to a building site.
Right? And because it's brick he needs a bigger truck than
usual. So he heads down to the yard, gets a cup of tea, has a
bit of banter in the canteen, collects his rig from the shed and
starts out. He's driving through the town for about five
minutes, sitting up high in the cab, bouncing along, and he's
just about to get on the bypass when he turns a corner and
there in front of him, there's a few fellas digging up the road.
Doing a bit of roadworks, you know? There's a bit of a
traffic jam as well – a car and a fella on a bicycle. But he's
not expecting this – there's those makeshift traffic lights and
they're red, you know? He's not expecting this so he slams
on the brakes, and just about stops without hitting anything.
He waits a few seconds and the lights turn green and off he
goes. Right?

KATE. ...

JOHN. So on he goes. He's driving for a while. The road's nice
and clear so he doesn't have to stop. Anyway, an hour or so
later he's pulling into the building site and there's a couple
of fellas hanging around. He waves at them to be friendly,
you know? But they don't wave back. They just stare at
him. They look at him like he shouldn't be there. Suspi-

cious, you know? He thinks he's in the wrong place and he begins to get worried. Because you used to hear stories of drivers ending up in the wrong building site in the wrong part of town, you know? So he decides to park up in a quiet part of the site, out of the way from all the fellas who are looking at him. He turns the engine off to have a look at his dockets and that, to make sure he's in the right place, you know? So he's hoking in his glove compartment and he hears something. A noise. So he sits still and he can hear someone crying. Weeping like a child. It spooks him out a bit, you know? He was that kinda fella. So slowly he opens the door and jumps down out of the cab. He walks around the front of the cab. Guess what he sees?

KATE. ...

JOHN. There. In the grill. Jammed in by the handlebars. Is the bicycle from the traffic jam. And the cyclist still on it.

KATE. Is that true?

JOHN. It's a story.

KATE. But it didn't really happen, did it?

JOHN. You said you wanted a story so I've told you a story.

Pause.

KATE. Where did you and Mum meet?

JOHN. What?

KATE. Where did you and Mum meet?

JOHN. What are you asking me that for?

KATE. Sorry, I'm just asking.

JOHN. You shouldn't ask me that.

KATE. Sorry, I just thought I'd ask –

JOHN. Why today?

KATE. What do you mean?

JOHN. Why are you asking me this today?

KATE. I don't know.

JOHN. Right.

KATE. Why not ask you today?

JOHN. Yeah.

KATE. What are you talking about now? You're not making any sense.

JOHN. …

KATE. I just thought I'd ask.

JOHN. Right.

KATE. So –

JOHN. Well, I might want to know something.

KATE. …

JOHN. I might want to know something.

KATE. What are you talking about now?

JOHN. I might want to know something.

KATE. I heard you – what are you getting flustered about?

JOHN. Did your mother say anything about me?

KATE. What do you mean?

JOHN. Did she ever say anything about me? Anything bad?

KATE. What are you asking me that for?

JOHN. I just want to know.

KATE. You're confusing me now.

JOHN. It's alright. I don't mind you saying. She must have, did she? She must have tried to tell you things about me.

KATE. I'm not going to answer that.

JOHN. She must have told you a few things to try and get you on her side –

KATE. Lies, you mean?

JOHN. Because there's two sides to every story –

KATE. You know what it is – ?

JOHN. I was thinking about –

KATE. You have too much time on your hands.

Long pause.

Eat your sandwich. Are you not going to eat your sandwich? 'Cause if you don't want it I'll take it.

Pause.

Are you finished there?

JOHN. …

KATE. Are you going to eat that rind?

JOHN. …

KATE *eats the rind then clears the plates.*

KATE *flicks on the kettle and goes about washing the dishes, etc.* JOHN *watches her.*

KATE. I broke my iron. Got it out this morning and for some reason it just wasn't working. I'm the only one who uses it so I have no idea how it broke. It was fine when I used it the last time. Do you know how long I've had it? Eighteen years. We got it as a wedding present from Sean's uncle.

Pause.

Do you want the radio on?

JOHN. …

KATE. Daddy?

JOHN. …

KATE. Is everything okay?

JOHN. …

KATE. Maybe you should go for a wee nap.

JOHN. I'm alright.

KATE. Are you sure?

JOHN. Stop talking to me like I'm a child.

Pause.

KATE. Maybe we could do some decorating in here. Give the place a lick of paint, brighten it up a bit before the winter really kicks in. Give the place a bit of life. Wouldn't that be good?

JOHN. …

KATE. Something modern. Magnolia or something. Wouldn't that be a good idea, seeing as you spend most of your time in here. We may as well have it looking good.

JOHN. …

KATE. We could even have two different colours. They do that now, you know, gives the feeling of space. It would be nice in here. Wouldn't it?

Long pause.

JOHN. Your mother made you that dress from old curtains that we had in the bedroom.

Pause.

I didn't know where you were. I came home from work and you were gone. I thought she'd taken you for a walk or something to the playground. Or you'd gone to your grandmother's. So I made something to eat, a cheese and ham sandwich and a cup of tea. And I sat on my own and ate it. I cleaned my dishes and put them away. I went into the living room and flicked through a few magazines. I didn't know what to do with myself in the house on my own. But it didn't happen often so I went upstairs and took my clothes off and had a bath. A bit of peace and quiet. And I was lying there in the bath and I don't know how or why but something clicked. In my head. I realised you were both gone. That she'd left and taken you with her –

KATE. Daddy, I know all this –

JOHN. She didn't leave a letter or anything like that. She didn't even do that but somehow I still knew. She'd just taken you and left. I went back downstairs and had a smoke. I stood staring out the window. And this is the thing. And I knew I wasn't going to try and find you. I knew I wasn't going to look for you. I knew she wouldn't want me to. You were both gone. Completely gone. Without another thought I decided to leave you both to it. I settled for my lot. It was easy. I went down into the town and got drunk. I came back home and went to bed.

Pause.

I always knew she wanted someone different to me. I always knew that.

Pause.

KATE. You've told me that before. You know that, don't you?

JOHN. …

KATE. I just want to know where you met each other. I was only asking. Because I don't know. So I was only asking.

Long pause.

JOHN *heaves a few times and swallows.*

KATE *begins getting ready to go.*

I have to head on now. Is there anything you want me to bring up tomorrow?

JOHN. …

KATE. Is there anything you want me to bring up tomorrow?

JOHN. …

KATE. Are you not talking to me now?

JOHN. …

KATE. Are you not talking to me now?

JOHN. …

> KATE *is on her way out the door.*

> Kate. I wanted to call you Aisling.

KATE. Why are you telling me that?

JOHN. Just.

KATE. That's a nice name.

JOHN. …

KATE. …

> KATE *exits.*

Scene Three

Late afternoon.

JOHN *takes the picture and mirror from the wall and places them behind the sideboard.*

JOHN. And when you catch a trout there's a flash in the water.
Where he twists and shows his belly really quickly.
When he knows he's been got.
Even at night you can see his belly when he flips over in the water.
Even at night – it's that white.
Some trout have been known to travel oceans.
Did you know that?
That's not normal for them usually.

But they know that now.
I don't know how they know but they know.
It's got to do with temperature I think.
It gets too cold for them so they strike out across an ocean
for warmer waters.
Thousands of miles of open water.

JOHN *arranges the contents of the tin box neatly on the*
sideboard.

It's just you and me now, huh?
Just the lads.
We might go for a walk later, huh?
Up to the mountain maybe.
Will we do that?

Pause.

You see all that rubbish I was saying earlier? – ignore it.
Ignore all of it.
I like the sound of my own voice sometimes.
That's all.
That's all that was.

Pause.

I was trying to say something useful.
Something you'll need to know.
But there's no point.
You think by now I'd know better.
You'd think by now I'd know that.
Huh?

Pause.

JOHN *sits on the bed.*

Do you think about her?
Do you?
Sometimes I think about her.
Sometimes I think about her.
And that first time I saw her.
In that dress she had.

Dancing.
She danced with half the fellas that night.
I didn't think I stood a chance.
But we danced.
And I walked her home.
Summer.
Warm.

Long pause.

JOHN *heaves once. He lies down on the bed.*

Remember the homeless fella standing outside the cathedral?
Where was that?

Pause.

A counting dog, huh?
What about that?
A counting dog.

He takes three breaths – not breathing out on the third breath.

Silence.

Through the window from outside, a car headlight shines on the corner of the bed.

The light moves up the adjacent wall and bends along the ceiling.

Silence.

The End.

LIMBO

Limbo was first performed by Sneaky Productions in the Queen's Drama Studio, Belfast, on 7 November 2005, with the following cast:

GIRL   Bronagh Taggart

Director   Owen McCafferty
Designer   David Craig
Lighting Designer   David McDonald
Producer   Jonathan Harden

Characters

GIRL, *late teens*

GIRL *in her late teens; dressed for a night out; standing by the shore of a mountain lake.*

GIRL. I think I've always had a fear of water.
There's something about it.
Besides being wet.
Don't get me wrong – I like water.
I drink it.
I wash with it.
But…

It was raining on the morning of my seventeenth birthday.
I went into work as usual.
John, the line manager, called me into his office.
You only get called in if you're stealing or fiddling your clock-in card.
John has the slowest voice in the world.
(*John.*) 'Youse wanna come in now?'
I felt someone behind me.
It was Shauna.
She was carrying a cake – candles and everything.
Estelle was there as well, Anne Marie and Lizzy, a whole crowd of them.
They started to sing 'Happy Birthday'.
I didn't know they knew.
The cake was one of those sponge ones you get in petrol stations.
It was lovely.
It was a complete surprise.

I'd been working with the girls for a few months – packing line in the meat factory.
The girls were older than me – mostly in their mid-twenties.
I think I was the youngest on the floor.
I remember that as a lovely day.

It would've been dull if they hadn't done that.

On the way home I missed the bus and had to walk.
I got completely soaked.
I got home and put the kettle on.
I thought about phoning home, but I didn't.
I peeled off my clothes and put them in the machine.
I showered and decided to shave my legs – why not?
I put on my dressing gown and read a magazine.
The doorbell rang.
It was the girls.
They had loads of drink.
They sat me down.
Shauna knelt down and held my hands.
(*Shauna*.) 'Right, I don't want you to say anything, but we've all had a whip around.'
(*Lizzy*.) 'We have.'
(*Estelle*.) 'Yep.'
(*Shauna*.) 'Here, we hope you like it.'
The box was velvet.
It was a silver necklace with a cross on it.
This one here.
Shauna started pouring drinks and Estelle got to work.
(*Estelle*.) 'Right, we have to get you ready. Isn't that right, Lizzy?'
(*Lizzy*.) 'That's right. We can't have her looking like that. I'll get my bag.'
(*Estelle*.) 'We are taking you to Oak and Chrome. Top spot. You're going to love it, isn't she, Shauna?'
(*Shauna*.) 'Yep. It's just opened. It's really nice. Swanky.'
(*Estelle*.) 'Shauna knows the doorman, don't you, Shauna?'
(*Shauna*.) 'Yep. Lovely fella, really down to earth – '
(*Estelle*.) 'Shauna's shagged him – '
(*Shauna*.) 'He's a lovely fella – '
(*Estelle*.) 'What are you going to wear?'
I didn't really have anything.
(*Estelle*.) 'Is your wardrobe in your room?'
Estelle ran up the stairs and I could hear her rummaging.
She came back down.

(*Shauna*.) 'Jesus, Estelle…'

(*Estelle*.) 'Like a glove!'

(*Shauna*.) 'You can't have her wearing that.'

(*Estelle*.) 'Why not?

(*Shauna*.) 'It's lime green!'

(*Estelle*.) 'That's the point… Shauna, is there any drink on the go or what?'

We drank.

Lizzy did my hair and made me up.

Of course, Estelle and Lizzy got louder and louder and when the taxi arrived Lizzy started flirting with the driver.

She told him she'd forgotten her purse and could she pay him some other way.

He asked her what she had in mind.

She told him, 'Fuck off, you're older than my dad.'

There was already a queue around the corner.

Shauna touched up her make-up and fixed her top.

She went up to the bouncer and whispered in his ear.

Then she kissed him on the cheek and put her hand in his pocket.

The place was jammed.

We found a corner and soon the table was full of cocktails.

And the girls were throwing them back.

I was trying to keep up but I wasn't used to it.

But I was trying.

The music got louder and louder.

Almost straight away Lizzy needed to go to the toilet so she took me with her.

I thought I saw blood on the bathroom floor but Lizzy said it was lipstick.

When we got back out into the club Lizzy ran ahead.

I was beginning to feel dizzy.

I looked up and I could see her head disappearing into the crowd.

I didn't see the step in front of me.

I stumbled.

Drink went everywhere.

Some mad bitch started to cry.

One girl, in a pink boob tube had drink the whole way down her front.

I started to laugh.

A man dressed in a fancy suit, sitting at the bar, got up and came over.

He put his hand on my shoulder and asked me if I was alright.

I couldn't stop laughing.

The man said I was with him and that he was sorry for the mess.

He bought the whole table a round.

It must have cost a bomb.

He didn't say anything.

Neither did I.

We just sat there.

Then he got me a glass of water.

I started to cry and I told him I was sorry.

'It's my birthday.'

He started talking.

He was in business.

He sold parts for car seatbelts.

He told me he was forty-five.

'It's my birthday.'

'You look like my uncle.'

He laughed.

But he looked nothing like my uncle.

I'd ask him where he was from.

He said I wouldn't know.

But he was staying in a B&B – over Camlough Lake.

'Very good,' I said.

He asked me if I was ever up there?

I said I probably was.

'The lake is beautiful at night.'

He smiled.

'Are you alone?'

I managed to tell him it was my birthday and I was with the girls.

'It was nice meeting you.'
I never shook a man's hand before.
Except once at a funeral.

I went back to our table.
Some other people were sitting at it.
I waited a few minutes then I looked for the girls in the
toilets, then in the back bar.
I wandered around – I couldn't find them anywhere.
The lights came on so I walked outside and sat on a kerb and
waited.
I waited until the cleaners closed the doors.

The town was empty.
I decided to go home along the river.
I walked for a while and my feet started to get sore.
By the time I got to the bridge they were killing me.
I saw a car coming towards me.
It slowed down and pulled up right in front of me.
The headlights were right in my eyes.
I remember thinking 'Ignore it.'
'Are you getting home alright?'
I remember thinking, right... another nutter... no problem...
stay calm... and run...
Then I heard my name.
'Claire.'
It was him... the man from the bar.
'Where do you live? I'll drop you off if you like.'
'I can't find the girls.'
'Listen, I can drop you off. It's no problem.'
'I better not.'
'You look freezing. It's no problem.'
'I better not.'

We drove along Francis Street, out onto Merchants Quay,
down to Sugar Island and up Canal Street.
We didn't say anything.
It started to rain.
The driver said that he needed to stop in a petrol station so
he pulled in.

And that was the first time I really had a good look at him.
He had bits of grey hair but only bits.
He kept looking at my chest then to my eyes and then looked at my lips.
He turned his head and looked up and kissed me.

The raindrops on the window met and ran down the glass.
The driver came back and we drove off.

I heard the taxi pull off as I hung up my coat.
There was a message from the girls on my phone.
They'd gone on to a party and Shauna pulled the bouncer again.
I went up to my room and got undressed.
I left my make-up on and climbed straight into bed.
He got in beside me and asked me if I was okay.

He was already downstairs when I woke.
It was around eight and he'd turned the radio on.
I decided to wear my white top.
He was smoking in the yard.
'Did I did wake you?'
I asked him if he wanted some tea.
'No,' he said. 'Let's go out for breakfast – my shout.'
The news came on so I turned the radio off.
He asked me if I liked living by myself.
I didn't answer him.
He finished his cigarette and came back inside.
'You really suit white, you know. Honestly.'
So we left and walked down Canal Street.
He kept asking me stuff: 'What's your favourite colour?'
'Who's your favourite actor?' 'Do you like singing?'
'Dunno, I've never thought about it.'
'Well, what's your favourite song... it can be anything.'
'Dunno... I've loads of favourites.'

We went to a café and had breakfast outside.
I had tea and toast.
He had coffee and crêpes.
When we were done he lit up a cigarette.

'Last night was good, wasn't it?'

I took another half cup.

We didn't really say anything.

We kept looking at each other.

It was weird and I was beginning to feel... silly... or something.

He lifted my hands and kissed them.

'I have a business meeting next week. I'll be staying in the same place. Maybe we should go to dinner?'

I wrote my number on a napkin.

'Sorry I have to go but I have to get out of the B&B by ten.'

He got up and put on his jacket.

'I wish I could spend the day with you.'

The taxi came.

He kissed me again.

I got home and made my bed... put on a wash... ran the bath...

He didn't call.

We went out every week after that – sometimes twice a week.

Mostly to Oak and Chrome.

Shauna was doing a steady line with the doorman... Mark.

Mark was there and he'd let us in for free.

There was another place called The Yard.

Then there was Baccus, and Dante's.

I'd blow my whole week's wages.

We always thought we were going to miss out on something if we didn't go out.

Once I was sick all weekend.

So I took the Monday morning off work.

And the Tuesday.

I ended up taking the whole week off.

I went back the following Monday, still a little ill, and of course John took me into his office.

'You'll be needing a doctor's note.'

And that set me off.

I started to cry.
I don't know why.
I just felt sad, and sorry.
Really, really... sorry.
He asked me what was wrong and I said it wasn't his fault.
He made me a cup of coffee even though I didn't want one.
He told me to go home.
He asked me if he should phone my parents...

And later, I remember sitting on the edge of the bath.
Waiting.
I waited.
I remember thinking I should just go for a walk – just to do
something.
I walked around the town for ages.
Somehow I ended up on a railway bridge, close to a church
and my old primary school.
I remember planting watercress when I was younger.
And I remembered mine was the first to grow because I was
closest the window.

Days went by.
Weeks.
I told no one.
And I went back to work.
Nothing really changed.
In fact most things were the same.

It was St Valentine's Day and we all went out.
There was a traffic-light disco and foam party.
We all sat together.
I was green.
Shauna and Mark were red.
Mark had some good-looking friends.
There is always someone acting the ass.
His name was Arron.
Proper rich kid – dressed like he didn't have the money.
He was taking pictures of everyone.
Whether they wanted it or not.
He just kept taking pictures.

That's all he seemed to do.
I tried to ignore him.

The foam came squirting out from a hose hanging from the
ceiling.
Before long the whole place was covered.
And with all the lights it was class!
People were slipping all over the place.
It was only a matter of time before someone made his way over.
It was Arron and this camera.
He was pissed.
'Aren't you sick of taking people's pictures?'
'I think the camera likes you.'
He started to dance beside me.
I think that's what he was doing.
Then he fell on the ground and I helped him up.
He put his arms around my waist.
He couldn't take his eyes off me.
I forgot about the camera.
He kissed me.
I surprised myself when I kissed him back.
We danced.
It was that simple.
He was a really bad dancer but he was laughing and sliding
all over the place.
He didn't care.
I took the camera from around his neck to take a photo of him.
He posed like Elvis.

When the lights came up we went to the bar.
Arron managed to buy us both a drink before it closed.
Two double sambucas.
We downed them.
We met up with the rest of the gang outside.
Arron said if were were up for it we could all go back to his.
We were.

There was plenty of drink.
Arron put on some dance music.
We sat there.

People started to doze so Arron said he wanted to show me
the other room.
We went up a set of wooden stairs.
He lit a candle... but it only half-worked...
The room was full of bookshelves.
There were cushions in the corner.
He put on some jazz.
He said this is where he comes when he needs his own
space.
'You've a really nice house.'

He told me he planned on travelling to Greece next year.
He showed me some pictures – he'd been travelling before.
There was one of him on top of a mountain.
I could come to Greece with him when he goes.
He said it would be fun.
He was really nice.

He said he liked my eyes.
But I knew he couldn't make out their colour.
I kissed him.
He had a tongue piercing.
I thought about the photo and how Greece was so far away.
I stopped kissing him.
He asked me what was wrong.
I said something about being tired.
He took off his jumper and gave it to me for a pillow.
He pulled out a blanket and put it over me.
'Goodnight.'
He smiled.
He turned the music down low... very low.
He left the candle burning... half a flame...

I told him about the baby.
I don't know why I told him.
But he was so nice.
I felt I could talk to him.
He smiled and held my hand under the blanket.
'All the more reason to sleep.'
I fell asleep listening to the music – jazz: John... somebody.

I woke up.

I was freezing.

For a second I forgot where I was.

I heard him breathing behind me and I saw the bookshelves.

And the candle had burnt down to its stump.

I lay there for ages.

I could hear the music from downstairs still playing.

I lay there for ages.

'Are you awake?'

'Yes.'

'Me too.'

I turned over and he was looking at the ceiling.

His hair didn't know if it was coming or going.

He asked me if I wanted breakfast.

We got up and went down the stairs.

There were bodies all over the place.

Arron asked them all if they wanted breakfast.

That seemed to wake them up.

Arron told them to follow us in.

We walked across the garden.

Just the pair of us.

Our feet got wet on the grass.

And his kitchen was enormous.

It was like something from a magazine or off TV.

There was a stove... an old one... and this massive table.

His mum was in her dressing gown eating toast.

She was beautiful.

She asked us how the night went.

Arron said it was great.

Arron introduced me.

She said it was nice to meet me.

'There's bacon already on the pan and there's plenty of bread.'

She said she had to get a move on but Arron's da was
hogging the bathroom.

She began to put on her make-up beside the window.

Me and Arron sat at the table and had bacon sandwiches
and tea.

I didn't realise I was so hungry.
We talked about what we drank, but we couldn't really
remember what we had.
I was going to check my purse to see how much money I'd
left, but then I decided it was a bad idea.
Arron put on more toast and filled the kettle again.
I heard someone come down the stairs.
It was Arron's dad.

She reacts.

His braces were down around his hips and he hadn't combed
his hair.
He was doing up his tie.
He looked at me and put down his collar.
He turned to Arron.
'Arron, have you seen my shoes!'
Arron said he didn't know.
He grabbed a cup of tea that had been sitting on the worktop.
He walked out and went back upstairs.
I felt sick.

Arron's mum put on her coat – she had her car keys in her
hand.
She asked me if I wanted a lift into town?
I got up.
Arron walked me out.
'We're all going out again next Friday if you wanna come.
Maybe we can meet up for a drink before?'
I think I nodded my head.
His mother got in and we pulled out of the drive.
I still felt sick.
'Where can I drop you off?'
I told her anywhere in town.
We reached the bypass roundabout and headed into town.
'And what school are you at?'
I told her I worked.
'That's the way to do it. In at the deep end is the only way to
learn.'
She kept driving.

'Where is it you live? I can drop you off. It's no bother.'
'Off Canal Street – the top end.'
We came in along the Dublin Road.
She turned into Dominic Street to avoid the lights.
We turned into Francis Street, out onto Merchants Quay,
down to Sugar Island and up Canal Street.
She said she loved the mornings.
I looked dead ahead.
She told me I was pretty and that she wished she was my age
again.
But I didn't cry.
We arrived at my house.
'It was really nice to meet you,' she said.
I don't know why I leant over and gave her a hug.
Or why I didn't let go.
But I didn't cry.
She asked me if I was okay.
I nodded.
I got out.
She waited until I was inside.
I stood in the hall.
And she waited in the car.
I thought she'd get out and ring the door.
Then I heard her put the car in gear and drive off.
I pulled off my clothes in the hall and on the stairs.
I went into the bathroom and was sick.

I took a shower and went to bed.
And stayed there all day.
I woke up that evening and tried the light.
There'd been a power cut.
I lay on the bed, the quilt around my chin.
My fingers were cold.
I could hear the mumble of voices in the room next door.
And some music.
I pulled the covers over my head and curled up.
I cradled my legs in my arms.
It was getting cold.
I heard something next door get knocked over.

I didn't want to cry.

I heard a door slam.

It was quiet.

Then for the first time I thought I felt a kick.

I waited.

Then I felt it again.

I decided I'd tell the girls I was expecting.

I wanted to tell them all together but I didn't want to tell them in work.

There's something not right about telling people you're having a baby when you're wrapping ham slices in plastic.

Then one Friday in work the girls had mentioned doing something that night.

It was eleven o'clock and I was sitting on my own when they landed over.

I decided to tell them tonight.

They were at their usual volume and Estelle had a few in her already.

(*Estelle*.) 'Shauna and Mark have split up. Isn't that right Shauna?'

She was sitting in the armchair, quietly getting drunk.

She didn't answer.

I didn't know they'd split up, but I knew she liked him.

(*Lizzy*.) 'So we're taking her out to get her drunk.'

(*Estelle*.) 'Although by the looks of it she doesn't need us.'

(*Lizzy*.) 'Plenty more fish in the sea and all that.'

(*Estelle*.) 'What about you and that Arron fella? He's always asking after you.'

Shauna reached over to pour herself another whiskey and Coke.

She saw I hadn't touched mine.

(*Shauna*.) 'He said to remind you that he'll be there tonight. Here's his number.'

He'd written it on a scrap of paper.

(*Estelle*.) 'That's right. A wee bit weird though, wasn't he...?'

Then Estelle stood up and so did Lizzy.

(*Estelle*.) '...so are you coming or not?'

I looked over at Shauna.

She was staring at the floor.

I wanted to ask her if she was okay but not in front of Estelle and Lizzy.

I told Estelle I wasn't feeling well and that I hadn't much money.

(*Estelle*.) 'Right, well, we're heading on or else we won't get in.'

I walked them to the door.

I was going to say something when they were on the doorstep.

But they were in a hurry to get into the club.

I didn't want to ruin their night.

I shouted after them, 'I'll see you on Monday!'

But they didn't answer.

Estelle and Lizzy were singing, arm in arm.

Shauna walked behind them.

They got to the end of the street and turned the corner.

I closed the door.

So I started reading books again.

I tried to save money.

I showered all the time.

My skin was cleaner.

My only craving was pistachio nuts.

As far as everything else was concerned, a baggy jumper did the trick.

And I didn't call Arron.

Another Wednesday after work.

I put the kettle on and I opened my post.

A bill and my rent receipt.

Shauna said she would call round but she didn't show.

So I made myself a salad.

With nuts.

I ran a bath and got in.

The baby began to kick but by now I'd grown used to it.

I lay there as still as I could.

And the water rippled every time it kicked.

Of course, the doorbell rang.
I got out and put on my gown and opened the door.
It was him.
He came in.

He asked me if I was okay.
I didn't answer him.
He looked into the living room and noticed Lizzy's cigarettes
on the mantelpiece.
He asked me if I smoked.
I looked right at him.
I should have said 'Fuck you!'
But I didn't.

He asked if he could sit down and sat down.
I closed the door.
I sat down.
He sat looking at me.
He said he was sorry.
Really sorry.
He didn't mean for all of this to happen.
I thought about him that time in the taxi.
He asked me if I was still working?
I said I was.
'Take time off,' he said.
He told me to quit.
There is no need for me to work.
'Don't worry about money,'
He reached into his pocket and took out his wallet.
'This will get you started.'

I went into the kitchen and made some tea.
'This is not that difficult to get through.'
He followed me into the kitchen.
'Listen, trust me. We'll take it one day at a time. It's best to
be realistic, don't you think?'
He took off his jacket and hung it over his arm.
'Did you ever think of getting rid of it?'
'No.'
'Of course not.'

I suddenly felt embarrassed that I was in my dressing gown.
As if it mattered.

I asked him about Arron and his wife.
'Arron was talking about you... he really likes you... he's
got his exams soon...'

We went back into the living room and he drank his tea.
I put on the radio, just to have something else going on.

I told him about when I found out.
I told him what weight the baby was inside me.
I told him when I was due.

'Have you any pictures from the scan?'
I reached down the side of the armchair and pulled them out.
They were inside a cardboard frame the hospital gave me.
He stared at them for ages.
He asked me if I knew what sex it was.
I did but I didn't say.
I wanted to keep something for myself.

'We have to stay friends. Don't we?'
I don't think he wanted to cry.
He turned around and hugged me.
Then his hand moved down over the baby.
I don't know how long we stayed in each other's arms.

At some point though he said he had to go.
He washed his cup in the sink and went to the door.
He opened it and turned around.
'Now get your bath and I'll see you soon.'
He ran his fingers down my face and tucked some hair in
behind my ear.
He left.

But he called.
Three times a week usually – sometimes four.
He bought me a TV.
He bought nappies and baby clothes.
He knew what to get.
He bought the shopping for me.

Nuts mostly.

I didn't leave the house.

I had an appointment with the doctor one Friday.

I was going to get a taxi and maybe take a walk into the shopping centre.

'No, you have to rest.'

He took me there, waited and took me back.

I wished I'd have walked – the fresh air would have done me good.

He painted the spare room for us to have as a nursery – two walls blue and two walls pink.

He bought me a home manicure kit.

I spent hours doing my nails.

He bought a high chair and some toys.

Then this happened.

He called over one Friday and it was late.

He'd had a long day at work and he didn't feel like going home.

I made him a cup of tea but he didn't drink it.

I sat down beside him.

He turned on the TV and fell asleep on the sofa.

I must have dozed as well because when I woke up I was lying in his arms.

It wasn't a hug or anything, but it was like…

'Are you awake?'

'Yes.'

I kissed him.

He kissed me back.

The baby moved so I sat up.

I felt a sharp pain and he asked me if I was alright and I said no.

He told me to breathe slowly so I did.

He asked me what I was feeling.

'I'm sore.'

I was sore.

Really sore.

He told me not to worry – things were fine.

He went to my bedroom and packed my bag.
We went out to his car.
I nearly tripped on the step.
He told me to slow down, everything was alright.
I told him to hurry up.
I got in and we drove to the hospital.
Slow – he drove so slow.
I could feel the baby moving.
He put on the radio.
'Music sometimes helps,' he said.
'Thanks.'

I went into the delivery room on my own.

He was waiting in the ward for me.
He had bought flowers and some magazines.
He took my hands and kissed them.
I asked if he wanted to hold her.
I didn't really want to let her go but I thought I'd have to at
some point.
He took her and went to the window.
He must have stood for fifteen minutes just looking out over
the town.
'From up here you realise how small this place really is.'
She was sleeping in his arms.
He didn't say much after that but it didn't matter.
He'd be up again tomorrow.

'Mother and child sleep well?'
We did.
He held my hand.
'While I was at the bedroom I gave the kitchen a lick of
paint as well – purple.'
He started playing with my fingers.
'And I've got some money set aside for her. We can set up an
account. Is that alright?'
I didn't ask him about Arron or his wife – it didn't seem like
a good time.

A few days later it was time to go home.
He came up to collect me straight after work.

He'd been working late and it was dark by the time he arrived.
He'd bought some chocolates for the nurses on the ward.
They were very fond of him.
As we got into the car he said he had an idea.
'We should go for a drive.'

He had her in his arms.
I looked back across the fields to the car.
I could barely see it in the dark.
We got down to the edge of the lake.
It was really beautiful.
He gave her back to me and lit a cigarette.
We stood there.
For ages.

'I have a problem. I mightn't see you for a while.'
'I've thought of a name for her. Aisling. I read it in a magazine. Do you want to know what it means?'
But I could tell he wasn't listening.
'Business is taking me away...'
He finished the cigarette and lit another one.
'I have a few things to do over the next few weeks... and I mightn't get to call by... you know?'

'It's best to be realistic, isn't it?'

'I have a job... a wife... and a family.'

I held her in my arms and stood there.
I didn't say anything.
I just stood there.
He finished his cigarette and stubbed it out on the stones.
'Come on, I'll drop you home.'
He walked back up toward the car.
I didn't know whether to follow him or not.
I stood with her in my arms and looked out over the lake.
He got in and started the engine and waited.

I looked out across the lake.
The water was black.

And calm.

The sky was clear.

And the reflections of a few stars were shining on the surface.

I heard the water in and around the reeds.

My feet were damp.

And I held her.

And I didn't cry.

And I tried to think about something else.

Lights down.

The End.

CATHERINE MEDBH

Catherine Medbh was first performed as part of 'The Miniaturists' in the Arcola Theatre, London, on 25 March 2007, with the following cast:

HIM   John Hollingworth
HER   Kerry-Jane Wilson

Director   Ciaran McQuillan

Characters

HIM, *late twenties/early thirties, unkempt*
HER, *late twenties/early thirties, well dressed*

Lights up.

HIM *and* HER *sitting in a bar.*

HIM *has a pint of Guinness.*

HIM. You get caught in that rain? No?

HER. No.

HIM. Ah good. Nice and dry. Good. Good. You're looking well.

HER. Thanks.

HIM. Yeah. Can I get you a drink?

HER. I'm not staying long.

HIM. Me neither. I just stopped in here for one, y'know? Wet the whistle. You don't want any crisps or anything?

HER. I'm not hungry.

HIM. Right. It's nice in here.

HER. It needs a lick of paint.

HIM. Ah. I dunno. I like it as it is. Character. Quiet. Plenty of time to yourself.

HER. Plenty of time to think?

HIM. Plenty of time to think.

Pause.

We'll get a bit of music going, will we? What have I got here? 20p, or is that a fifty? What is that?

HER. Just leave it.

HIM. Yeah?

HER. I'm not really in the mood.

HIM. No. You're right.

HER. There mightn't be anything you like. Just leave it.

HIM. Aye. I'll just leave it.

Pause.

I like your hat. You. Bought. That. In. Galway.

HER. I didn't think you'd remember something like that.

HIM. Oh yes. You know me. You only wore it the once though, if my memory serves me right.

HER. No.

HIM. No?

HER. I probably wore it more than once.

HIM. I only saw you wear it once.

HER. I probably wore it when you weren't around.

HIM. Yeah. Probably yeah. You're wearing it now though.

HER. Yeah.

HIM. And it's still nice. Are you sure I can't get you anything?

HER. No. Thanks.

HIM. Righto. Well, there you go now. There you go.

Pause.

So. You still teaching?

HER. Yeah.

HIM. It suits you, y'know? You a teacher. Not that you couldn't be anything else. We both know you have brains to burn. But no. Teacher is you. I always thought it was…

HER. What?

HIM. Ach. You know what I'm going to say so –

HER. What?

HIM. Ach, you teaching. Going out in the mornings with your hair wet.

HER. What?

HIM. It was kinda sexy, y'know?

HER. Yeah?

HIM. Ach, you know it is. That wee dress you used to have, huh?

HER. Oh yeah. That one.

HIM. Ah come on. You knew what it did for me.

HER (*smile breaks through*). I don't know what you mean –

HIM (*smiling*). Ah. See. Huh? You were a vixen back then. Probably still are. Are you?

HER. …

HIM. Ah now. There you go.

Pause. They catch each other's eye.

So how's married life?

HER. Great –

HIM. Actually don't answer that one.

HER. No?

HIM. Nah. Sorry. Sorry. I shouldn't have – I'll shut up.

Pause.

HER. How's work?

HIM. Actually, funny you should ask.

HER. Why?

HIM. I quit today.

HER. Did you?

HIM. I did. I did. I quit my job today. The boss was a cock.

HER. What happened?

HIM. Ach. It was more a mutual agreement, y'know? I turned up late a few days in a row. He got a bit arsey.

HER. Right.

HIM. Aye. It's not like he…! Like all he had to do…! Suppose he's doing his job, y'know?

HER. Yeah.

HIM. Strangely though, I'm not down at all. I feel good, y'know?

HER. Yeah?

HIM. Yeah. A weight off my shoulder or something. It's hard to explain. But it's. A weight off my shoulder. Nothing holding me down, y'know? I can see – I can see things clearly. It's all opening up, y'know? Nothing on top of – horizons! New horizons in front of me and all around. Open road. No more nine to five, it's just the open straight – the home straight. Y'know?

HER. That's good.

HIM. Yeah. You gonna ask me what I'm going to do now?

HER. What are you going to do now?

HIM. Well, this is it, you see. I've been thinking about setting up my own wee business.

HER. Doing what?

HIM. Ah now. Can't say. That would be shooting myself in the foot. No, I'm just going to keep that one close to my chest if that's alright. Don't want to count the chickens, y'know?

HER. Yeah.

HIM. Don't want to put an omen on it. Not immediately now. It'll be a while. But – well, you'll see. Meantime, I'm just taking a bit of time to myself. Gather my thoughts. Get everything – together.

Pause. They catch each other's eye.

What?

HER. What?

HIM. Were you going to ask me something there?

HER. Me?

HIM. Aye. You looked like you were going to ask me something.

HER. No.

HIM. No?

HER. No.

Pause. HIM *takes a drink.*

HIM. Do you mind if I ask you something?

HER. Depends what it is.

HIM. Eh. Right. Well, it's nothing bad. It's not. It's just a general question. It's just curiosity. Right?

HER. Right.

HIM. Well. And the reason I'm asking is because I was walking about there this afternoon and all the children were coming home from school and that. 'Cause when you're working shifts you forget there's children going to school. You do. You forget about those wee things, y'know? Anyway. I saw them all coming home getting picked up by their mas and das and – and it just got me thinking about, y'know? About all that. So. Well, so. Well. I was wondering. Do you ever think about...

HER. What?

HIM. Well. You're probably going to have children now with your new fella and that.

HER. I dunno.

HIM. I know that. I don't mean to say you will. 'Cause you mightn't. But I was just wondering if you ever think about what happened. Y'know.

HER. Sometimes.

HIM. Right. Right. That's alright. And what do you think?

HER. I try not to think about it.

HIM. Right. Of course. Yes.

HER. It was a long time ago. It just wasn't meant to –

HIM. Now before we go any further. You have to know. I didn't leave you because of that. You know that, don't you? I was just feeling weird. I don't know. We were young, y'know? Still are. It was just something I had to do. Move on. I don't even know why. I just know I felt it. And. Well. It had nothing to do with what happened. I need you to know that. I do. I really need you to know that. Y'know?

Pause.

Did you have a name for him?

HER. Who?

HIM. Him. It. Whatever.

HER. It was a her.

HIM. Oh. Right. Sorry. Did you have a name for her?

HER. No.

Silence.

HIM. Guess who I was talking to at the weekend there?

HER. Dunno.

HIM. Try.

HER. Dunno.

HIM. I met him in here.

HER. …

HIM. Nelson Mandela.

HER. And how is he?

HIM. The best. The very very best. Asking me how I was. Asking me how everything was going. Great fella. Big table-tennis fan, y'know? Good at cards. Nice man. Nice man. Now, it wasn't actually Nelson Mandela. Not the actual man. It was all in my head, y'know what I mean? Like it wasn't actually him. He wasn't there. But. He may as well have been. Y'know –

HER. So what was he saying?

HIM. No. You're missing my point. You see this is the thing. This is the thing. I was here talking away to myself, right? In this very chair. Right. We've established that. But I managed to talk to Nelson Mandela at the same time. Do you know what I mean? Are you following me? You know what I'm getting at?

HER. Yeah.

HIM. And I didn't feel ashamed. I didn't feel stupid talking to him. I probably looked like a mentalist, talking away to myself. But it didn't matter. I was where I was and that was that. It was actually quite nice. Catching up with him, y'know?

HER. Yeah.

HIM. Good. Good. As long as we're all singing from the same hymn sheet.

Pause.

We never danced enough. Didn't we not?

HER. No.

HIM. Yeah. We thought about it though.

HER. We had a free lesson once.

HIM. That's right. What was – ?

HER. Charleston.

HIM. Correct. That was good fun, wasn't it?

HER. Yeah.

HIM. Sweating like a pig. I really liked it though – despite my 'reservations'. Still remember some of the moves, y'know?

HER. Yeah?

HIM. Oh yes.

Pause.

Aye.

Pause. HIM takes a drink.

I've done nothing but natter on and on. Excuse my manners. You know what I'm like. I get all –

HER. Social.

HIM. Indeed. Social. You!

HER. What?

HIM. You talk to me now. Give my wee tongue a rest. I've done nothing but talk shite. You talk to me now.

HER. What do you want me to say?

HIM. Anything. Say anything. It'd be nice to hear your voice.

HER. Yeah?

HIM. What can I say, you've a nice voice.

HER. What should I say?

They catch each other's eye. Hold. Long pause.

I know you left because you were lonely. I know you wanted to talk about it, but felt you couldn't. I know you wish it was different, but you don't know how. I know you still love me.

Pause.

I know you thought turning on the light would wake me up. I know you put your clothes on in the kitchen in case you made too much noise. I know you boiled the kettle to make yourself a cup of tea. I know you decided against it. I know you turned off the heat. I know that you found a pen and tried to write me a letter. But I know you didn't know what to say. I know you went into the living room and looked out the window. You watched a fox canter down the street. It vanished into a ditch. I know you noticed the TV was on standby so you switched it off. I know you tidied the papers on the coffee table. I know you tied your shoes in a double knot. I know you felt your way down the hall. I know you nearly tripped on my brown boots. I know you didn't cry. And I know you saw my scarf hanging on the door. And you touched it. You buried your face in it. You tried not to think of me. You put the scarf in your pocket. I know you left your keys on the phone table and opened the door. It was barely dawn. I know you stepped out into the morning and I know it was cold. You closed the door. And I know you didn't cry. I know that.

Pause.

HIM. Tell me you love me.

HER. I love you.

HIM. Say it again.

HER. I love you.

HIM. And again.

> HER *mouths the words 'I love you.'*
>
> HER *disappears. Pause.*
>
> HIM *goes to drink but doesn't.*
>
> *He takes three deep breaths.*
>
> *The End.*

Other Titles in this Series

A Nick Hern Book

St Petersburg and other plays first published in Great Britain as a paperback original in 2008 by Nick Hern Books Limited, 14 Larden Road, London W3 7ST, in association with The Bush Theatre, London

St Petersburg, *Limbo* and *Catherine Medbh* copyright © 2008 Declan Feenan

Declan Feenan has asserted his right to be identified as the author of this work

Cover image: Lorna Ritchie
Cover design: Ned Hoste, 2H

Typeset by Nick Hern Books, London
Printed and bound in Great Britain by Biddles Ltd, King's Lynn

A CIP catalogue record for this book is available from the British Library

ISBN 978 1 84842 033 5

Mixed Sources

Product group from well-managed forests, controlled sources and recycled wood or fiber
www.fsc.org Cert no. TT-COC-002303
© 1996 Forest Stewardship Council